REALLY WICKED

GOLF JOKES

REALLY WICKED

GOLF JOKES

Compiled by David Brown

MICHAEL O'MARA BOOKS LTD

First published in Great Britain in 1998
by Michael O'Mara Books Limited
9 Lion Yard
Tremadoc Road
London SW4 7NQ

A CIP catalogue record for this book is available from the British Library

ISBN 1-85479-376-4

1 3 5 7 9 10 8 6 4 2

Cover design by Powerfresh

Designed and typeset by Design 23

Printed and bound in Great Britain by Cox & Wyman, Reading, Berks.

GOLF

IS

RELIGION

A man went to confession and said to his priest, "Forgive me, Father. I used the F-word this week."

"Ah, my son," said the priest "Tell me the circumstances which caused you to use the F-word. After all, I can sometimes understand a person being provoked into using it."

"Well, I was golfing," said the man, "and I had just hit a beautiful tee-shot that sailed straight as an arrow for 250 yards, but then suddenly veered off into the woods."

"That is when you used the F-word?" said the priest "I can appreciate your frustration my son, as I am a golfer myself."

"No, I stayed calm at that point, Father," said the man. "I then hit a perfect shot out of the woods, but suddenly it landed in the sand trap."

"Now, I can understand you saying the F-word at that point," said the priest

"No, Father, I remained calm even then," said the man. "I got out my sand wedge and hit a perfect shot out of the trap right at the pin, but suddenly the ball stopped an inch from the cup."

"Ah, that is when you used the F-word. How frustrating," said the priest

"No, Father, I was still calm at this point," said the man.

"Don't tell me you missed the f**king putt?" said the priest

A keen golfer goes to his priest and asks him if there are any golf courses in heaven. The priest says he'll find out for him. The next day, the priest calls the golfer and says, "I've done some checking up and I've got some good news and some bad news. The good news is that there are golf courses in heaven and they're far better than any golf courses we have down here."

The golfer says, "So what's the bad news?"

And the priest says, "The bad news is that you've got a teeing-off time for next Monday afternoon.

Despite his considerable age, the Bishop was still a formidable golfer and he regularly trounced the Rural Dean.

"Never mind," the Bishop consoled him, "you have many years in which to improve your game. My future is limited – you'll bury me one day."

"Yes, Bishop . . . but it'll still be your hole."

Satan, fuming, called a staff meeting. Hell had become too soft an option due to the fiends' idleness and complacency, so he ordered every little devil to smarten up their acts and crack down hard on the guests. "I want them tested to the limit," he snarled, "tortured, tormented, humiliated and with the added twist that you must hold out a false promise that things will get better."

"Like in a game of golf?" a fork-tailed junior devil suggested, eager to show he had got the idea.

Satan, taken aback, spluttered "Hang–on nothing THAT strong, old boy. They're only human and, don't forget, they have to last out for all eternity!"

Father Patrick, who was not averse to berating his congregation for abusing the Sabbath, still occasionally snuck off to play a quick round of the course before the early morning service. At the crack of dawn, one summer morning, he was spotted on the tenth tee by an angel, who was extremely annoyed.

"Father, you must punish that wretched hypocrite," he said, as he reported the sinner to God.

"He will be punished, my son – watch this!" God replied.

Father Patrick hit off on the 590 metre, par five hole and his ball arced gracefully in direct line with the pin. It dropped onto the green and a gentle breeze took it and carried it the last few centimetres right into the hole.

The angel was astonished and said to God, "I thought you were going to punish him, Lord, but you've given him what every golfer dreams of– a hole-in-one on the longest hole of the course."

God smiled at his angel, "I HAVE punished him, my son. Who on earth can he tell?"

While playing golf, a man finds a corked bottle on the green. Upon opening it, a genie appears and grants the man one wish. After pondering for a while, the man says, "I'd like to shoot par golf regularly."

"No problem," says the genie, "but you must understand that your sex life will be greatly reduced as a side effect."

"I can cope with that," the man says, and WHOOSH! the deed is done in a puff of blue smoke.

A few months later, the genie reappears on the same golf hole and asks the man how his golf is going.

"Fantastic!" says the man, "I'm now carrying a scratch handicap."

"And what effect has it had on your sex life?" the genie inquires.

"I still manage to have relations a couple of times a month," the man answers calmly.

"A couple of times a month," the genie says, "that's not much of a sex life."

"Well," the man responds, "it's not bad for a middle-aged priest with a very small parish."

Jesus and St Patrick were out on the back nine one day when the sky began to darken and a thunderstorm started to rage. Amidst the roaring of the thunder and the cracks of lightning, Jesus turned quickly to St Patrick.

"This storm looks dangerous," he said. "We'd better get in before one of us gets hit by the lightning."

"There's nothing to worry about," said St Patrick, casually going over to his bag and pulling out an iron. "Just stay close to me," he said, and he headed off down the fairway holding the iron up over his head.

"Are you crazy?" cried Jesus. "You'll be killed."

"Nonsense," said St Patrick. "This is a one iron. Not even your father can hit a one iron!"

Moses, Jesus and a little old man got together for a round of golf one day. When they came to the first of the par threes, which happened to be about 150 metres with a carry over a pond, Moses hit first. He hit a low grounder that headed right for the water. When the ball got to the edge, the water miraculously parted and the ball rolled right through the pond and up on to the green.

Next it was Jesus's turn. He got up and hit almost the exact same shot as Moses, except that when the ball reached the pond it simply rolled across the top of the water and up on to the green.

Now it was the little old man's turn and, you've guessed it, he went ahead and hit the same shot as the other two, except that his shot rolls to a halt just in front of the water. All of a sudden, a fish pops its head out of the water, picks up the little old man's ball, swims across to the other side with it and spits it out onto the green. Then, out of the blue, a rabbit appeared. The rabbit proceeded to pick up the ball in its mouth, hop over to the hole and drop it into the cup for a hole in one.

As the three of them head down the fairway, Jesus turns to the little old man. "Nice shot, Dad."

A group of blind people are playing a round of golf. Naturally enough they are going round quite slowly. Behind them are a priest, an imam and a rabbi. The priest says, "What a marvellous achievement to see them overcoming their disability."

The imam says, "Much as I'm humbled to see these people doing what they're doing, I do wish they could go a bit faster," and the rabbi says, "What, they can't play at night?"

After church one Sunday, one of the congregation went up to the priest and said, "Father, is it a sin to play golf on Sunday?"

"My son," said the priest, putting his hand on the man's shoulder, "I've seen you play golf. It's a sin any day."

Back at the nineteenth, in a vile mood, he delivered his bitter tale of woe.

"Nothing could stop me winning. I had a putt of about eleven inches, hardly more than a tap-in, to clinch it. The green was dead flat, perfectly true, a real billiard table. Not a breath of wind.

My ball was heading for the cup, on rails. Then a raven swooped down, snatched it up, and circled the flag stick twice. The raven passed the ball to a vulture, which flapped to Paradise Brook, opened its talons and . . . splash. End of Story."

St Peter sighed deeply and vowed, "Last time I ever play St Francis of Assisi."

HUSBANDS AND WIVES

For several months, Jenny had been nagging her husband Bob to take her to the country club so she could learn to play golf. He finally agreed, and off she went with a set of clubs. That afternoon, Jenny walked into the bar, grimacing with pain.

"So, did you enjoy your game of golf?" Bob asked.

"It was horrible," Jenny replied. "I got stung by a bee."

"Where?"

"Between the first and second holes," she said.

"Sounds to me," Bob replied, "like your stance was too wide."

•

Mike and Jane were beginning a game of golf

Jane stepped up to the tee, and her first drive gave her a hole in one. Mike stepped up to the tee and said, "OK, now I'll take my practice swing, and then we'll start the game"

•

"It's true," the weekend golfer told his wife on his way out of the door, "I love golf more than I love you. But," he proclaimed, "I love you more than tennis."

A husband and wife are playing golf together when one day they come upon a par 4 hole. The husband hooked his drive deep into the woods and proclaimed that he would have to chip it out.

"Maybe not, dear! said his wife. "Do you see that barn over there, if I open both doors on both sides, I do believe that you could hit it right through and onto the green!" So the husband agrees to give it a try, but when he hits the ball, it goes straight through the first doors but hits the crossbeam and ricochets back, hitting his wife and killing her.

About a year later he is playing a round on the same course with a fellow member and hooks the ball deep into the woods again. Just as he is about to chip the ball out, his partner rushes up to him and says "Do you see that barn over there? If I open both doors on both sides, I do believe that you could hit it right through and onto the green!" "No way," replies the man, sadly, "I tried that last year and got a seven!"

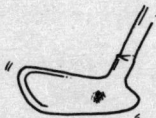

Colin Robinson was a rather henpecked husband. In fact, the only time he managed to get away from it all was at the annual school reunion where, each year, a trophy was awarded to the man who told the funniest story about making love to his wife. This particular year, Colin won it and proudly took the trophy home.

"What did you win that for?" demanded his wife.

"Er, it was, er... it was for telling a story about when we played golf on holiday last summer, dear," Colin stammered in reply.

"Hurrumph," grunted his wife and wandered off. The next day she bumped into the wife of another man who had been at the reunion dinner.

"Hello, Mrs Robinson," said the woman. "I gather that your Colin won a prize for telling the best story at the dinner last night."

"Yes, but I've no idea why," replied Mrs Robinson. "We only did it once. His cap blew off, he couldn't get it in the hole and he lost the ball."

Wife to Husband: "How did your golf game go today, dear?"

Husband to Wife: "Fine. I played with our dentist, Dr Blackmore."

Wife back to Husband: "Oh, that's nice. How does he play?"

Husband back to Wife: "He plays well enough, except he has this annoying habit of continually walking over to the cup on each green and saying "Would you open a little wider please?"

Arthur and Bob were playing a round of golf the other day and, just as they were about to tee off, a funeral procession went by.

Arthur put his club down, took off his cap and bowed his head as the cortège passed.

"That was a very decent gesture," said Bob.

And Arthur responded, "It was the least I could do. She was a damned good wife to me."

Wife: "You think so much about golf all the time, I bet you don't even remember when we got married."

Husband: "Of course I do, dear. It was the day I sank that twelve-yard putt."

"I haven't seen my husband for ten years," the wife said.

"Be patient," advised her lawyer. "Maybe he's taken up golf."

First man: "My wife told me this morning that if I don't give up golf she'll leave me.

Second man: "That's bad luck."

First man: "I know, I'm really going to miss her.

When Jayne's husband arrives home from the golf course several hours late, she demands an explanation.

"We had a problem," he said. "Ken collapsed and died on the second hole and from then on it was play the ball, drag Ken, play the ball, drag Ken..."

Through the first four holes of the golf course, Bob was very quiet. Finally, on the fifth tee, Barry asked, "What on earth's the matter, Bob? You haven't said one word."

"It's my wife," Bob replied. "Ever since she's been working overtime at the phone company, she's cut our sex down to twice a week."

"You're lucky," replied Barry. "She's cut me off completely."

"Shut up, Judy!" shouted the angry golfer at his nagging wife. "Shut up or you'll drive me out of my mind!"

"That wouldn't be a drive," snapped Judy in reply, "that would just be a putt."

As they left the church on the way to the reception, the groom turned to his bride saying, "I've got a confession to make, darling, I adore golf. I eat, sleep and breathe golf. I'm totally obsessed with golf and I have to tell you that it completely dominates my life."

The bride smiled sweetly at him and said, "Thank you for being so honest with me. Now, I also have something important to tell you – I'm a hooker."

"No problem," the groom replied, taking hold of her wrists. "You hold your left hand just a little higher than the right, with your thumb down here . . . . "

A young golfer was about to get married and two days before the happy event, he was hit in the groin really hard by a golf ball.

"Sorry, son," his doctor told him, "but your tackle will have to go in a splint."

On his wedding night, his young bride strips off and points at her breasts. "Aren't they beautiful?" she asks him, "and never touched by human hands."

The young man pulled down his underpants and, pointing at his crotch, says, "That's nothing, mine hasn't even been unpacked."

"So, how did it go at the golf course today?" the man asked his heavily-pregnant wife as she came in the door.

"It went great," she replied. "I played so well that when I walked off the eighteenth green, I actually felt the baby applaud.

After dessert, the women stayed around the kitchen table to chat, while the men went into the living room to talk. Soon the conversation in the living room turned to the subject of golf.

"What was your best score?" one of the men asked another.

"Let me find out," he said, as he got up and started to head towards the kitchen.

"Where are you going?" the others asked him.

"To find my wife," he replied. "She's the only one who remembers what I've been telling people."

There was a hold – up at the short eleventh hole and just as they were about to play off, a man rushed off the tenth green.

"Excuse me," he called out, "but would you mind very much if I played through? I've just heard that my wife has been taken seriously ill."

When the golfer returned home after his long day out on the links, his wife asked, "How did it go today, Bill?"

"Well, I was great at hitting the woods, for what it's worth," Bill replied.

"That's excellent, darling, well done!" she exclaimed.

"Yes, really well done," Bill said sarcastically, "now all I've got to do is learn how to hit out of them!

Mike and his secretary were having an affair. One day they decided to leave the office early and go to the secretary's flat for an afternoon of lovemaking. Afterwards, they fell asleep and didn't wake up until 8pm. They quickly got dressed and Mike asked his secretary to take his shoes and go and rub them in the grass. The secretary thought this was pretty weird, but she did it anyway.

When Mike finally arrived home his wife was waiting for him at the front door. She was clearly very upset and asked him where he had been.

Mike replied, "I cannot tell a lie. I'm having an affair with my secretary. We left work early, went to her place, made love all afternoon, and then we fell asleep. That's why I'm late!"

His wife looked at him, noticed the grass stains on his shoes and said, "You lying bastard. You've been playing golf again, haven't you?"

Chris came home one day from playing in his local golf tournament. "How did it go today?" his wife asked as he came through the door.

"Not very well, I'm afraid, Ian had to be taken off to hospital in an ambulance."

"Heavens! Chris, that's awful! What happened?"

"He was having a rotten day." said Chris. "He kept missing shot after shot and the more he missed the more angry he got. Finally, he got himself into such a state that he ruptured a blood vessel and passed out completely."

"That's really terrible," said his wife.

"I know it is," said Chris. "It gives a whole new meaning to the term 'Stroke play.'"

The day after her husband's untimely death, the widow, Mrs MacDonald met with the funeral director.

"What would you like to say in the obituary?" he enquired.

"MacDonald died." she replied.

"Don't you think that's a bit abrupt, Mrs. MacDonald?" the funeral director queried. "Isn't there anything else you might like to add?"

"Oh, all right," she said, "How about, 'Macdonald died. Golf clubs for sale.'

A husband and wife were on the ninth fairway at their local club, about to hit their approach shots to the green, when all of a sudden out of the blue, a golf ball came whizzing past them, missing the husband's head by a fraction of an inch. A minute or two later, a woman came over from the next fairway looking to retrieve her ball.

"Are you mad?" said the wife. "You hit a lousy shot like that and you don't even have the courtesy to shout 'Fore.' You know, you almost hit my husband!"

"I'm so terribly sorry." the woman apologised, holding her club out to the wife. "Here, do take a shot at mine."

"I'm absolutely sick to death of being left alone every weekend while you go out and play golf," grumbled the golf widow to her husband one fine morning during breakfast.

"If you think you're going off to play again today, you've got another think coming!"

"Don't be ridiculous, darling," replied her husband.

"Trust me when I tell you that golf is the last thing on my mind. Let's just finish this argument once and for all. Oh, and would you mind passing the putter?"

CADS AND CADDIES

Golfer: "This is a terrible golf course. I've never played on a worse one."

Caddie: "But this isn't the course! We left that more than an hour ago."

Phil and Tony had arranged a game of golf at the club. When they met up at the first tee, Phil was surprised to see Tony standing there with not one but two caddies by his side. They teed off and were about half-way around the course when Phil could not contain his curiosity any longer.

"What's this then?" asked Phil. "Did you win the lottery or something?"

"What do you mean?" asked Tony.

"You know what I mean," said Phil. "The two caddies. Why are you using two caddies?"

"Oh, them," said Tony. "My wife was complaining I wasn't spending enough time with the kids."

Golfer: "I've never played this badly before."

Caddie: "You've played before?"

Golfer: "That can't be my ball, caddie. It looks far too old."

Caddie: "It's a long time since we started, sir."

Golfer: "What a disastrous round. You must be the worst caddie in the world!"

Caddie: "I doubt it, sir. That would be too much of a coincidence!"

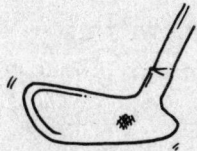

After a series of disastrous holes, the strictly amateur golfer, trying to smother his rage, laughed hollowly and said to his caddie: "This golf is a funny game."

"It's not supposed to be," said the caddie gravely.

A well known pro golfer hits his drive deep into the woods for the third time that day.

"The number four axe I think," he says with aplomb while turning to his caddie.

"I'd move heaven and earth to be able to break 100 on this course," sighed the elderly golfer.

"Try heaven,"advised his caddie, "You've already moved most of the earth.

The man was standing in the witness box of a court. "Have you ever taken the oath?" asked the judge. Then, noting the quizzical look on the man's face, added, "Do you know how to swear?"

"Oh yes, sir," he replied, "I'm your caddie."

The golfer and his caddie had been out on the course for what seemed like forever. After more than several hours had passed, the caddie began spending what, to the golfer, seemed to be an inordinate amount of time looking at his watch. The man was becoming annoyed at his caddie's actions and finally spoke up.

"I just want you to know," said the man, "that I'm aware that I'm not the world's greatest golfer. But even so, I've taken the whole day off work and I'm just going to relax and enjoy myself, no matter how long it takes to finish. So you can stop constantly looking at your watch."

"I fully appreciate that, sir," said the caddie, "but this is not my watch, it's a compass."

Few people carry a heavy burden further than golf caddies.

Colin was having a dreadful game and just seemed incapable of hitting the ball right. The caddie was teetering towards breaking point and it finally came after forty strokes or so at the sixth hole.

"What should I take for this one?" Colin asked innocently.

"Beats me," growled the caddie. "Seems like a toss up between a cyanide capsule or the next train out of town!"

The hacker came upon a hole that was famously said to possess the world's largest fairway bunker. Naturally, his tee shot, as if drawn by a magnet, found its way right into the heart of this monster. As they reached the abyss, the hacker peered over the edge and turned to his caddie.

"What club do you suggest?" he asked.

"Well, sir, it doesn't really matter much," the caddie replied, "but may I suggest that you don't go in there without an adequate supply of food and water."

The miserly old skinflint met up with his caddie, who he rather resented having to employ, at the first tee. The caddie placed his bag down and handed him his driver.

"Before we head out," cracked the old guy, "I want to know something. How good are you at finding lost balls?"

"As it happens, sir," replied the caddie, "I take great pride in my ability to find lost balls."

"Well then, what are you waiting for?" snapped the old guy. "Get out there and find one so we can get going!

"Look, that's it!" said the exasperated golfer to his insolent young caddie. "I've had enough of your cheek and I'm going to report you to the caddie master as soon as we get back to the clubhouse."

"Yeah, yeah," responded the youth, "I'm really worried now."

"You should be worried." said the golfer.

"Oh yeah, why's that?" said the youth. "At the rate you play, by the time we get back it'll be time for me to retire anyway."

After hitting his tee shot deep into the woods, the hacker turned to his caddie.

"Did you see where that one went to?" he asked.

"No, sir, as a matter of fact I didn't." replied the caddie.

"Why on earth didn't you watch where it went?" snapped the angry golfer.

"Frankly, sir," said the caddie, "I was totally unprepared for it to go anywhere."

The lady golfer was a determined, if not very proficient player. At each swipe she made at the ball, earth flew in all directions.

"Goodness me," she exclaimed red-faced to her caddie, "the worms will think there's an earthquake."

"Oh, I don't know," replied the caddie, "the worms round here are very clever. I expect most of them are hiding underneath the ball for safety."

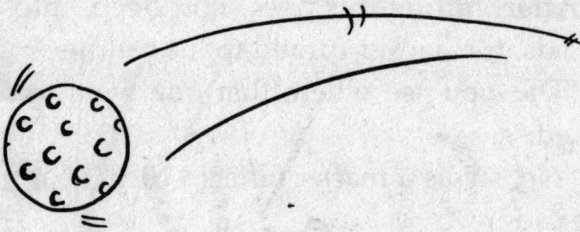

THE
LADIES'
GAME

Two women who hadn't seen each other in a while ran into each other in the car park at their golf club the other morning.

"So what's new?" asked the first woman.

"I just got a brand-new set of golf clubs for my husband," the second woman said.

"Sounds like you got a pretty good deal," said the first.

The women were in the kitchen listening to the men going on and on in the next room, talking about nothing but golf and sex.

"You know," said one of the ladies, "it's amazing how at their ages they can spend so much time talking about golf and sex."

"What's so amazing about it?" said another. "At their ages, about all they can do is talk about it."

Two merchant bankers' wives were about to tee off at their golf club one morning when one turned to the other and said, "Tell me, darling, before we head off, shall we play by the men's rules . . . or does every shot count?"

A golf professional, hired by a big department store to give golf lessons to interested customers, was approached by two ladies.

"Do you wish to learn to play golf, madam?" he asked one of them.

"Oh no," she replied, "It's my friend here who's interested. I learnt last Wednesday."

Two women were put together as partners in the club tournament and met on the putting green for the first time. After introductions, the first golfer asked, "What's your handicap?" "Oh, I'm a scratch golfer," the other replied. "Really!" exclaimed the first woman, suitably impressed that she was paired up with her. "Yes, I write down all my good scores and scratch out the bad ones."

Vicky and Jenny were playing a round of golf one sunny morning. Jenny teed off and watched in horror as the ball headed directly toward a foursome of men playing the next hole. The ball hit one of the men, and he immediately clasped his hands together at his crotch, fell to the ground and proceeded to roll around in agony.

Jenny rushed over to the man and started to apologise. She then explained that she was a therapist and offered to help ease his pain. "Please allow me to help. I'm a physical therapist and I know I could relieve your pain if you'd just allow me!" she told him earnestly.

"Aargh . . . oooh . . . nooo, I'll be alright . . . I'll be fine in a few minutes," he said, remaining curled up on the ground with his hands still clasped together at his crotch.

But she persisted and he finally allowed her to help him.

She gently took his hands away and laid them to his side, loosened his trousers and put her hands inside, beginning to massage him.

"Does that feel better?" she asked.

"It feels great," he replied. "But my thumb still hurts like hell."

The learner woman golfer came storming into the clubhouse after making a hopeless attempt to play a round.

"I don't believe it!" she said angrily. "What an incredible drag. All that time and money for nothing. Those f**king lessons were a complete waste of time—I still can't play golf worth a damn!"

"Excuse me!" said one of the other members, interrupting her in mid-flow. "I couldn't help overhearing you, but if you don't mind my saying so, it might have been more helpful if you'd taken golfing lessons instead!"

The golf pro took the novice woman player out to the practice range for her first lesson.

"The first thing you need to do," the pro said, taking a golf ball out of his pocket and holding it up to her, "is tee the ball."

"Look here," she snapped. "Let's get one thing clear right now. Just because I'm a woman and I'm new to the game, there's no need for you to be condescending, so let's just cut the baby talk right now."

True golfers' adage: Give me a set of clubs, a great golf course to play on and a beautiful woman—and let's hit the links. She can keep score.

A man was playing golf and sliced his ball into the cow pasture. He crossed the fence and started looking for the ball. He noticed that there was a lady golfer, apparently looking for a ball too. He looked around and saw a cow staring at him reproachfully. He looked at the cow, but thought she couldn't possibly know anything about his missing ball. He searched and searched and the lady kept looking too. Eventually he approached the cow and lifted her tail gingerly. Sure enough there is a ball lodged in her backside. It doesn't look like his so he calls to the lady, "Hey does this look like yours?" The headline next day read, 'Woman kills man with a nine iron.'

WORDS

OF

WISDOM

Explorer: "There we were surrounded. Fierce savages everywhere you looked. They uttered awful cries and beat their clubs on the ground..."

Weary listener: "Golfers, probably."

Andy Johnson was walking on the golf course one day when he was struck on the head by a golf ball. Angrily, he demanded £500 compensation from the golfer who had driven the shot.

"But I said 'fore'," said the golfer.

"Done," said Andy.

An old man was watching a game of golf for the first time.

"What do you think of it?" asked his friend.

"It looks to me," he replied, "like a harmless little ball chased by men too old to chase anything else."

He plays a fair game of golf - if you watch him.

A golf ball is a golf ball no matter how you putt it.

Messing up yet another shot, the golfer whimpered, "There can't be worse players than me."

"There are," his partner assured him, "but they're not playing any more."

Last week I missed a spectacular hole - in - one – by only five strokes.

Golf is OK. It makes some of the best people take showers.

You can always tell the golfer who's winning. He's the one who keeps telling his opponent that it's only a game.

A shipwrecked golfer had made the best of his tiny island. When a cruise liner spotted his distress signals and sent a boat to investigate, the landing party was amazed to find a crude but recognizable nine-hole course which the castaway had played with driftwood woods, whalebone and coral putter and balls carved out of pumice stone.

"That's quite a layout," remarked the officer in charge of the landing party.

"You're very kind. It's rather basic," the rags-clad golfer responded. Then he smiled slyly and added, "But I am quite proud of the water hazard..."

Definition of a golf ball: A small object that remains on the tee while a perspiring citizen fans it vigorously with a large club.

Did you hear about the golfer who killed the Puerto Rican?

He shot a hole in Juan.

Nothing counts in a golf game like your opponent.

Golf is a lot of walking, broken up by disappointment and bad arithmetic.

Very proud of having walked around the course with him for the first time, Daddy's Little Sweetheart couldn't wait to tell everyone about her experience. "My Daddy is the best golfer in the whole world," she proclaimed. "He can play for hours and hours and hardly ever lets the ball go into one of those little holes."

When ground rules permit a golfer to improve his lie, he can either move his ball or change the story about his score.

Q: What should you do with your asshole before you have sex?
A: Drop him off at the golf club.

The headmaster was presiding at his school's Sports Day, while a celebrity guest waited to present the prizes. The head droned on through his standard set of clichés about the parallels between sport and adult life awaiting his pupils. Sportsmanship was precious, he said, and would earn success and respect in every sort of job, just as it did in any sport the boys could imagine.

"Obviously not a golfer," thought the VIP.

Two friends were sitting at the bar one evening talking about the sports they liked to play.

"I love to play golf," the first man said. "I think it's the best sport."

"No way," said his friend.

"I have a big problem with golf. There's something about it that's just not natural."

"Not natural?" the first man said. "Golf not natural? How on earth could you possibly say something like that?"

"The way I see it," said his friend, "is that there's something just not quite right about a game where the person who gets the most hits, loses!"

The difference between learning to play golf and learning to drive a car is that in golf you never hit anything.

Joe sliced his tee shot way off into a field beside the golf course. Finally, he found the ball nestled in some buttercups. On his back swing he heard a voice say, "Please don't hurt my buttercups." Joe stopped his swing, looked around, saw no one, and prepared to hit again. "Please don't hurt my buttercups," came the voice again. He stopped again, looked up and saw a beautiful woman approaching. "I am Mother Nature," she said. "If you promise not to harm my buttercups, I can guarantee an abundant supply of butter for the rest of your life."

Joe thought for a moment or two and said, "Where were you last week when I hit the ball into the pussywillows?"

His victim had been caught off guard and drawn into some serious–money betting. The golf hustler moved into top gear and started playing like a master. Aware of the dupe's suspicion, the hustler feigned surprise at his own miraculously improved form, shrugged modestly and muttered, "Somebody up there must like me."

"I hope so," snapped the burly sucker, holding his driver in a menacing manner, "because if I lose, you're likely to meet Him."

Two friends were having a drink in the clubhouse discussing equipment when the subject of woods came up.

"In my view the best wood in my bag is my five wood– it's got me out of trouble more times than I care to remember," said the first golfer.

"Oh no, I have to disagree," said his friend. "The best wood in my bag has got me out of more trouble than all the five woods on the planet ever could."

"Which wood is that?" the first man asked.

"My pencil!"

The hacker met his playing partners on the first tee.

"What's your handicap?" one of the men asked.

"My golf game!"

Two friends who hadn't seen each other for a while bumped into each other at the local golf course.

"Hi!" said the first friend, "You're looking great - have you lost weight?"

"Well, thanks for noticing," said the second friend. "I have, actually. I've been on that new golf diet. Perhaps you've heard about it?"

"No, as a matter of fact I haven't," said the first friend. "How does it work?"

"It's really simple," replied the second friend. "You just live on greens!"

What do alligators wear when they play golf?

Sportshirts with little middle - aged men on them.

"Did you know that Shakespeare was a golfer?" asked one golfer to another.

"No, I had no idea he was a golfer."

"Well, it happens to be true - I'm surprised you don't know that famous line of his."

"Which famous line is that?"

"You must know it. Haven't you ever heard of 'Putting is such sweet sorrow'?"

What's the real reason your golf pro is always telling you to keep your head down?

So you can't see him laughing at you.

A few golfers are chatting in the bar one day after a round of golf, and one of them says he sometimes takes his dog with him when he goes out to play.

"Whenever I get a bogey, my dog does a backflip." he adds.

"Really? How extraordinary!" say the others.

"Yes, and when I get a double bogey, he does two backflips!"

"Well, that's amazing!" they say. "How does he do it?"

"Easy," he says, "I kick him twice."

A golfer named Joe was paired with one of the club's good players, and he was anxious to get some free advice. Hitting first, he swung awkwardly and topped his drive. "Do you see anything I can correct?" he asked. "I see you're standing too close to the ball," the other remarked. "After you hit it."

Two little bugs were crossing a fairway on a golf course one sunny day, when they came across a golf ball. Just as they were about to go around it, they felt the earth beneath their feet begin to shake. As they looked up they saw the golfer approaching, and started to panic. Fearing for their lives, one bug turned to the other.

"Oh my God," he squeaked, "we're going to get squashed! I don't want to die. What are we going to do?"

"We need to find a safe place where we won't get hit." said the other bug. "Quick, quick! Climb up on the ball!"

DOCTOR DOCTOR

His doctor told him to play thirty – six holes a day, so he went out and bought a harmonica.

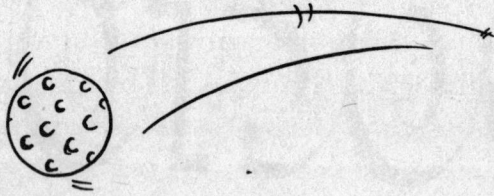

A dentist was right in the middle of working on a patient when the phone rang. Picking it up he listened for half a minute and then said,

"Yes, yes, I see. Don't worry,

I'll be right over." Hanging up the phone, he quickly removed his mask and gloves, went over to a cupboard, grabbed his golf clubs and rushed out of the office. "Good heavens, Doctor," exclaimed his astonished nurse, "What's happened?

Where are you going?"

"It's an emergency!" replied the dentist, as he raced through the door. "I have eighteen cavities to fill!"

A man was brought in to the accident and emergency department of a major London hospital one day, almost at death's door. He had somehow managed to get a golf ball lodged deep in his throat. He was immediately rushed into an operating room where a dedicated team of surgeons and throat specialists tried to save his life by removing the ball. After some tense hours the surgery was over and the operation was declared a complete success. The chief surgeon came out into the waiting room to find a man anxiously pacing up and down with three overflowing ashtrays beside him.

"Are you a member of the family?" the doctor asked him.

"No," replied the man, "But it's my ball."

First man: "My doctor has told me I can't play golf."

Second man: "So he's played with you too, has he?"

When the Maharajah of Merchandani was taken suddenly ill during a holiday in England, he was attended by a young locum filling in for the Harley Street surgeon. The Maharajah's appendix was deftly removed and the patient was overjoyed.

"You have saved my life," he said to the young man. "Whatever you want shall be yours."

"It was quite simple really," protested the young doctor.

"But I am a very rich man, I insist," said the princely patient.

"Well, I would love a new set of matched golf clubs," the young doctor admitted.

"Consider it done," came the stately reply.

Several weeks went past and the doctor had forgotten all about this grand promise until one day he received this cable:

"HAVE YOUR CLUBS BUT SADLY ALL NOT MATCHED STOP FOUR DO NOT HAVE SWIMMING POOLS STOP."

"God dammit, George, you surely don't expect me to pay that?" The two golfers were discussing a bill that George, the hospital administrator, has sent to Richard, a recent father for the first time.

"I mean, George, £35 for the use of the delivery room. It's just not on, old chap. You know I didn't get the wife there in time and the baby was born on the hospital's front lawn."

George leant over, took the bill, crossed out the offending entry and substituted another.

"Greens Fee, £35," it read.

Kevin loved playing golf but he had one small problem: every time he stood over a short putt he became flatulent. The weird thing was that whenever he became flatulent it would sound exactly like the word 'Honda.'

One day he went to Japan on a business trip and, following a successful meeting, he was invited to play a round of golf with his Japanese associates. Although he felt rather nervous because of his problem, it would have been insulting to refuse and so he accepted.

Sure enough, on the very first green, his problem became evident, and, as usual, it sounded just like 'Honda.' Overcome with embarrassment, Kevin began to apologise, when one of his partners said, "No need to worry – we can give you the name of a doctor in Tokyo who will be able to help you."

The following day he visited the doctor in Tokyo who, after being told of the nature of the problem, said, "Just get up onto the examination table here. I'm sure I can fix you right up."

After a lengthy examination the doctor exclaimed, "Ah, I know what your problem is – you have an abcess."

"What on earth does an abcess have to do with my condition?" asked Kevin.

"Don't you know?" said the doctor, "Abcess makes the fart go Honda!"

An elderly gentleman golfer lived on the third floor of a retirement home, next to the golf club. He used the path across the course as a short cut to the supermarket each day. One day, he was returning from the supermarket with a paper carrier full of groceries when he saw a stack of brand new golf balls beside the path. Unable to resist temptation, he emptied out his groceries and filled the bag. Unfortunately the ground was wet where the sprinklers were watering the greens and the damp paper burst, spilling the balls. Patiently he collected them all up and stuffed his pockets with them. As he waited for the lift, back at the retirement home a lady stood beside him and looked curiously at his bulging pockets.

Embarrassed, the old boy mumble, "Golf Balls," by way of explanation.

"Oh my," said the lady "Is that like tennis elbow?"

A golfer was taken to hospital suffering from sunstroke. The nurse began to read his temperature: "102 – 103 – 104 –"
"Hey, Doc," whispered the patient. "What's par for this hospital?"

SERIOUS GOLFERS

Irritated by his manager's request for yet another day off, to attend the funeral of his fifth or sixth grandmother – death always seemed to strike the family during the Open – the boss grumbled, "I do wish you cared as much about your work as you do about golf."

Shocked into honesty, the manager replied, "No way, Sir, I could never take work THAT seriously!"

Two golfers sliced their drives into the rough and went in search of the balls. They searched for a long, long time without success, while a dear old lady watched them, looking very sympathetic.

At last, after almost an hour, she came over to them and said, "Excuse me for interrupting you, gentlemen, but would it be cheating if I were to tell you where they are?"

The foursome teed off on the long par three eighth hole. The green on this particular par three lay behind a large bunker, so any shot that made the green would vanish over the bunker and it was impossible to tell where your ball had landed until you arrived on the green. After the last player hit his shot, the first player rushed off down the fairway, without waiting for his friends. He disappeared over the bunker and seconds later came rushing back down the fairway towards them, jumping and shouting, "I don't believe it, I don't believe it! I got a hole-in-one!"

"Come off it," said one of his friends, "you can't expect us to believe that. You run off ahead of us down the fairway and then disappear over the rise where you know we can't see you, and all of a sudden you've got a hole-in-one . . . . how stupid do you think we are?"

"No, no, it's true. I swear it's true," the first player cries, crossing his heart. "Go and look for yourselves – I knew you wouldn't believe me, so I left it in the hole to prove it."

A handsome young golfer was playing in his first professional tournament. At the end of the first day's play, the novice was ahead, and a beautiful woman sidled up to him in the clubhouse.

"Gosh", she cooed, "do you swing as well off the green?"

Rising to the challenge, he took the girl back to his hotel room and they made love, after which he rolled over and went to sleep.

"Hey," she shook him awake, "Tom Watson wouldn't give up so quickly!"

Mustering his energies, he made love to her a second time, after which he slipped off, quite exhausted.

The woman shook him again. "Hey, Arnold Palmer wouldn't fade away so soon!"

The young golfer summoned up his final remaining energy and made love to her yet again. When he was through, he fell asleep on top of her, too tired to move. She tapped him on the shoulder.

"Hey, Jack Nicklaus wouldn't just fizzle out like that!"

Angry, and a little mortified, the golfer got up. "Say – just what is par for this hole, anyway?"

First man: "It's hard to believe that old Harry is dead. And to think that he was going to play golf with us tomorrow. It's awful!"

Second man: "Yes, it's tragic! But wait a minute ... maybe we can get Mike to fill in for him."

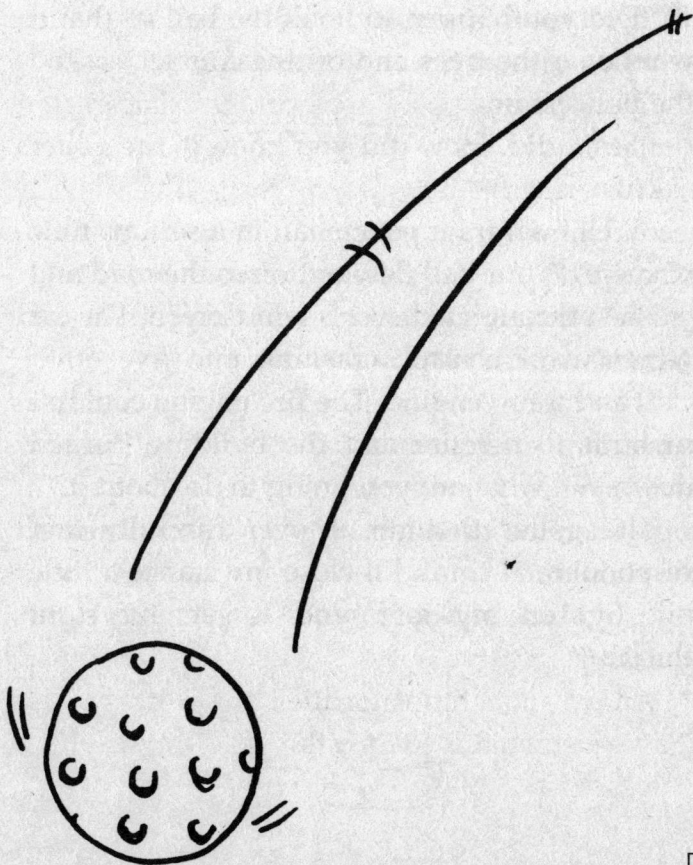

After a particularly poor game of golf, a popular club member skipped the clubhouse and started to go home. As he was walking to the car park to get his car, a policeman stopped him and asked, "Did you tee off on the 16th hole about 20 minutes ago?"

"Yes," replied the golfer.

"Did you happen to hook the ball so that it went over the trees and off the course?" asked the policeman.

"Yes, I did. How did you know?" the golfer asked.

"Well," said the policeman in a serious tone of voice, "your ball flew out on to the road and crashed through a driver's windscreen. The car went out of control, crashing into five other cars and a fire engine. The fire engine couldn't make it to the fire and the building burned down. So, what are you going to do about it?"

The golfer thought it over carefully and responded, "I think I'll close my stance a little bit, tighten my grip and lower my right thumb."

It was the first golfing day of the new season and Pete couldn't wait to get out on the course. He had spent the whole winter practising indoors, working on his swing and his putting. He had even invested a small fortune to go to one of those fancy golf schools for an intensive two weeks of one-on-one tuition, and he was ready.

He headed out with his caddie and, around about the sixth hole, he turned to the caddie, who, up until then, hadn't had much to say, and, puffing his chest up with pride, said to him, "So, tell me, have you noticed anything different since last year?"

"Yes, sir. I certainly have," said the caddie.

"And what's that?" Pete asked smugly.

"You've had your clubs regripped."

Two old boys were playing golf. After one particularly long and arduous hole, one turned to the other and asked, "So, how many did you take?"

"Nine," came the reply.

"Well, I took eight," said the first, "so I guess that's my hole then."

After the next hole, which proved to be equally time-consuming, the same old boy turned to his friend and asked the question again.

"No, no," said his friend. "It's my turn to ask first"

One day at the golf club, Bob spots the most beautiful woman he's ever seen in the clubhouse. Unbelievably, she comes over and suggests they play a round together.

She turns out to be a very fine player and gives Bob a good game, after which they go back to his place for some oral sex.

The following day they meet up for another game, followed by another bout of oral sex. This goes on for the whole week, at the end of which Bob says, "I'm sorry, but I don't think I can keep this up much longer."

"That's OK," says the woman. "There's something I have to tell you as well. I'm a transvestite."

"Damn!" exclaims Bob. "And all week you've been playing off the ladies' tees."

Tom came into the clubhouse one Sunday afternoon sporting a big black eye.

"What happened to you?" asked one of his friends.

"Have you noticed that beautiful buxom young blonde who has just joined the club?" Tom asked.

"Sure, who hasn't?" said his friend.

"Well, I happened to be standing by the first tee when she came over and took the cover off her clubs."

"So?" said his friend.

"I told her it looked like she had a really nice set."

One day the club duffer challenged the local golf pro to a match, with a £200 bet on the side.

"But," said the duffer, "since you're obviously much better than me, in order to even it up a bit, you have to let me have two 'Gotchas'."

The pro didn't know what a 'Gotcha' was, but he went along with it. And off they went. Coming back to the nineteenth hole, the rest of the club members were amazed to see the golf pro paying out £200 to the duffer.

"What happened?" asked one of the members.

"Well," said the pro, "I was teeing up for the first hole, and as I brought the club down, the crazy man stuck his hands between my legs, and grabbed my balls and shouted 'Gotcha!' Have you ever tried to play 18 holes of golf, waiting for the second 'Gotcha'?"

The other afternoon Jan called Sally in tears.

"He's left me, he's left me," Jan sobbed over the phone.

"What are you getting so upset about?" said Sally. "The worthless jerk has left you countless times before, and every time he comes crawling back, so what's the big deal?"

"This time it's different," cried Jan. "He's left me for good. He took his golf clubs!"

Simon was having a really bad day on the golf course. Just around the fourteenth hole he had just missed one putt too many. He let loose with an impressive string of profanities, grabbed his putter and stormed off towards the lake by the fifteenth tee.

"Oh dear," said his caddie to one of his playing partners, "there goes that club . . . "

"You think so?" said his partner, "I'll bet you a fiver he misses the water!"

After putting himself into the woods with his tee shot on the par three hole, the hacker looked over his second shot. He had to get the ball through the woods, over a group of trees, past a water hazard and a huge bunker, and land the ball on a severely sloped green.

Turning to his caddie he asked,"What do you suggest for this shot?"

"How about a prayer book?" came the reply.

Nick had a pretty bad day out on the links. It seemed like every shot he took, he either sliced or pushed the ball. All day long, slice or push, push or slice. Even the putts. He was pretty disgusted with himself and when he got home, he threw his clubs into the garage and went into the kitchen where his wife was having a cup of coffee.

"So, how did you play today?" she asked him.

"All right," he said.

An obsessional golf player was out on a first date with a very beautiful woman, and naturally he soon turned the conversation to golf. He spoke for a long time about the different courses he had played on, the precise kind of equipment he used, and gave detailed examples of different shots he had played in his time. To his delight his date sat quietly, drinking in his every word and smiling in agreement at everything he said. He couldn't believe his luck: not only was he out with this fabulous woman, but she actually shared his love of golf. It just seemed too good to be true.

"Anyway," he said finally, "Enough about me. Let's talk about you, I want to know all about you. How long have you been playing golf?"

"Golf?" she asked. "What's golf?

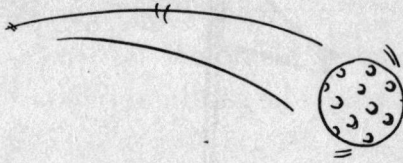

A golfer on a golfing holiday in Florida was playing a course where the sixteenth hole was a par three with an island green.As they arrived on the tee, his caddie said, "Did you know that Tiger Woods played this course only last week?"

"Did he really?" replied the golfer, as he teed up his ball.

He took his swing and watched the ball sailing through the air only to drop twenty yards short of the green straight into the water. "Damn!" he said to himself and teed up another ball. He swung again and watched the ball sail up into the air and splash back down into the water.

This time he swore out loud as he teed up his third ball. He took his swing and once again watched miserably as the ball flew up into the air only to splash back down in the water.

Turning to his caddie he said, "That's it. I give up. Tell me, what did Tiger Woods use when he played this hole?"

"An old ball," the caddie replied.

An American tourist was on holiday in Scotland and decided to stop by one of the local clubs for a round of golf. Being alone, he was paired with one of the local members, and as they were on their way down the twelfth fairway the American noticed a foursome on an adjoining fairway who were all wearing black armbands.

"What's all that about?" he asked.

"Oh, that's Malcolm's foursome." said his partner, taking off his cap and putting his hand over his heart. "Och aye, it's a very sad time indeed. Poor Malcolm recently lost his golf ball."

A foursome is teeing off on the first hole when one of them looks at the one about to tee off and notices something unusual.

"That's a peculiar looking ball you've got there, Anthony." he says, "What kind is it?"

"Well, it's absolutely the latest in ball technology." Anthony replies. "It's made of a special kind of space-age composite material so that it always seeks out the cup. It has a built in bleeper that goes off when it lands, and a built in light that goes on automatically at sunset, so it is impossible to lose."

"Wow, that's incredible!" says his friend. "Where on earth did you get it?"

"I found it!"

An English professor who was teaching at an American university was invited by a member of the college golf team to come out and play golf for the first time. They arrived at the course and the professor asked the student, "What do I do?"

"You have to hit the ball towards the flag over there on the green," the student explained.

So the professor carefully teed up his ball and proceeded to drive it straight down the fairway. The ball rolled onto the green where it came to a stop less than an inch from the hole.

"Well, what do I do next?" he asked the amazed student.

"You're supposed to hit the ball into the cup." he said.

"Oh, great!" exclaimed the professor. "Now you tell me!"

Golfer to partner: "I'm really anxious to make this shot, that's my mother-in-law up there on the clubhouse porch."

Partner to golfer: "Don't be ridiculous. It's well over 300 yards. You couldn't possibly hit her from here."

Two friends were out on the course one day. One of them was not having a good game and, by the twelfth hole, he had lost all the golf balls he had in his bag. Undeterred, he simply began using his friend's balls and continued having no success. As he went into his friend's bag for about the fifth time, his friend had had quite enough.

"If you don't mind," the friend said, "how about being a little more careful with your shots? These balls cost more than two pounds each."

"Listen," he snapped, "don't complain to me. If you can't afford to play this game, then you have no business being out here.

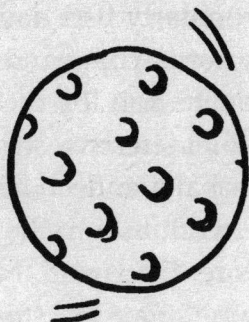

The sky above was blue and cloudless. Only a light breeze ruffled the treetops outside the window. If the judge had been a lawmaker instead of a law interpreter he knew he would make laws forbidding court sessions on such glorious days.

"Well," he mused, dragging his attention back to the courtroom, "I guess there's no way out. I might just as well tune back in on the case."

"And in addition to that, Your Honour," the barrister for the defence was droning, "my client claims she was beaten insensible by a golf club in the hand of her husband."

"How many strokes?" murmured the judge absently.

George had a particularly bad day on the golf course – nothing went right and he became more angry with every hole. By the 17th he was beside himself and let stream a string of curses the like of which has never been heard. George proceeded to toss his clubs into the lake and set his golf trolly on fire. Declaring that he would never play the game again he stomped off to the changing rooms and proceeded to cut his wrists.

At that point a fellow member wandered in and not noticing George's desperate condition, said "Hey George, we need a fourth for tommorrow morning, How about it?"

George looked up and said "What time?"

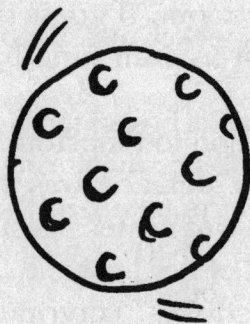

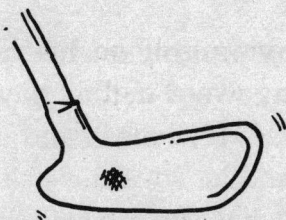

A man stranded on a desert island is amazed to see a gorgeous female scuba diver walking out of the water in a very low cut wet suit. He runs to greet her, as he hasn't seen another human being for 5 years. "Sounds like you could use a drink", she says as she unzips one of her pockets and offers him a flask of twelve-year old Scotch.

"That's the best drink I've ever had" says the man.

"Would you like a smoke" she purrs as she unzips another pocket and produces a hand-rolled cuban cigar.

"This must be the best cigar in the world" he exlaims as he blows a smoke ring into the air.

Slowly she starts to unzip the front of her wet suit. and says with a wry smile "Would you like to play around?"

"Have you got clubs in there too!", cries the man.

A man was playing golf on his own, but he played in a funny way. First he played the ball, then he kicked it a few yards and then played again and so on.

A fellow golfer watched this for some time and then could not resist asking him why he was playing in this curious fashion.
The golfer replied
"I'm playing a foursome with my wife!"